ICY HOOVES

Tiffany Pressler

ISBN 978-1-956696-00-4 (paperback)
ISBN 978-1-956696-01-1 (hardcover)
ISBN 978-1-956696-02-8 (digital)

Copyright © 2021 by Tiffany Pressler

All rights reserved. No part of this publication may be reproduced, distributed, or transmitted in any form or by any means, including photocopying, recording, or other electronic or mechanical methods without the prior written permission of the publisher. For permission requests, solicit the publisher via the address below.

Rushmore Press LLC
1 800 460 9188
www.rushmorepress.com

Printed in the United States of America

A little girl named Kaia dreamed of a white pony. She wanted a pony more than she wanted ice cream or cupcakes and more than Barbie dolls or stuffed animals. She had her heart set on not just any pony, but a white pony. She had dreams of riding this equine she had yet to find.

She was a horse-crazy little girl. She already had a miniature pinto horse named Sugar, but Kaia was growing so fast and was getting too big to ride her. She needed a larger pony so she could have new adventures at her grandparents' ranch.

Kaia had this wish for as long as she could remember, so one day, she took out her snow globe with a white pony inside, one that she had dreamed of, shook it, and wished for a white pony.

For months, her grandmother, an equestrian herself, searched and searched for the perfect white pony. She found quite a few ponies for sale—some big, some small—and there were many colors, but not white. So, she kept searching throughout the country from coast to coast. She did not give up because she knew that somewhere, she would find the perfect white pony for her granddaughter.

Kaia was taking English riding lessons at a nearby ranch. The riding instructor had a few ponies for sale, but not a white pony. After Kaia's riding lesson, she tried out a few of the ponies that were for sale. There were a buckskin and a sorrel pony for sale. Kaia tried them out and rode them around the arena, but they were not the white pony she dreamed of owning someday.

As Kaia and her grandmother were leaving the ranch after her riding lesson, they spotted a white pony in the stable. It was not just any pony but a white show pony right down the street in her hometown.

The problem was he was not for sale. Kaia's grandmother was determined and asked the owner of the ranch if she could buy this beautiful white pony for her granddaughter. The owner of the ranch said it did not belong to her, but to one of her friends that was keeping her horses and ponies there.

Not long after, the owner of the ranch contacted Kaia's grandmother and said that her friend was willing to sell the white pony to them. He was white as snow, half Andalusian and half Welsh pony. This majestic pony's Spanish name Guapo means handsome in English. This fancy little pony was born in Guadalajara, Mexico.

Kaia was overjoyed when she found out the search for a white pony was over. She and Guapo instantly became best friends and had many adventures ahead of them.

One of the favorite things she enjoyed doing was braiding his mane and placing colorful ribbons in it. Once she saddled him up, she would ride him around the ranch looking for fun things to do. One chilly evening, they trotted to the edge of the ranch near the lake to see the sunset. Kaia queued him to stop so they could watch the sunset. She noticed the lake was frozen over and thought about how fun it would be to ice skate with her pony. She turned him back toward the ranch and galloped toward the barn. She groomed and fed her pony and went home.

The next morning, she remembered to bring her ice skates to the barn. She took Guapo out of his stall and got him ready to go for a ride. He bowed his head and dipped his shoulder low so she could climb aboard. She grabbed a handful of his mane and swung her leg over. She lightly taped her heels into his side and he dashed off through the pasture fence and their journey began.

At the edge of the ranch, near the lake, Kaia eagerly jumped off Guapo and laced up her ice skates. She put one foot on the ice and glided across the lake like an ice princess. Guapo was right behind her slipping across the ice not nearly as graceful as his new friend. "Come on, Guapo," she called out. "Relax your knees and glide."

He started spinning and slipping. She reminds him that he is a dream pony and can do anything he sets his mind to. "Never give up," she called out.

"It's okay, Guapo," Kaia said. "Let me help you straighten your legs and get those icy hooves moving." She held his bridle while he gained confidence on the ice and the pair skated around the ice gracefully.

After the duo twirled around the ice, Kaia stepped off the lake to take a break. However, there was a problem. Guapo's hooves were frozen from the ice and the more he kicked and thrashed around, the more the lake became unstable and started to crack. He would soon fall underwater.

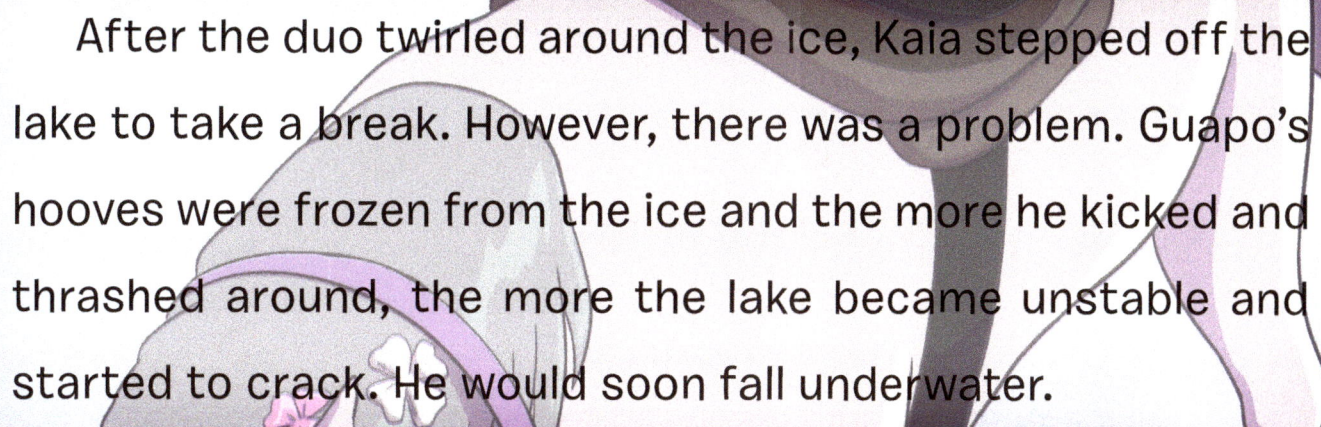

Guapo heard them and looked up as the ice cracked behind him. He made it to the edge just in time before the ice collapsed. Guapo's barn mates, Sugar and Montana, a black Quarter horse, realized he was in distress, so they ran to the edge of the pasture whining to him.

Kaia was thankful Guapo made it to the edge safely. She led him back to the barn where she put his blanket on to warm him up and gave him his favorite treat. She whispered in his ear, "What's our next adventure?"

www.ingramcontent.com/pod-product-compliance
Lightning Source LLC
Chambersburg PA
CBHW061107070526
44579CB00011B/173